ON THE RUN
True Stories of Legendary Outlaws

The Story of
JESSE JAMES

LINDSEY LOWE

T0054320

Enslow PUBLISHING

Published in 2024 by Enslow Publishing, LLC
2544 Clinton Street
Buffalo, NY 14224

Portions of this work were originally authored by Tim Cooke and published as *Jesse James*.
All new material this edition authored by Lindsey Lowe.

Children's Publisher: Anne O'Daly
Design Manager: Keith Davis
Designer: Lynne Ross
Picture Manager: Sophie Mortimer

Manufactured in the United States of America

CPSIA compliance information: Batch #CSENS24: For further information contact
Enslow Publishing LLC, New York, New York at 1-800-398-2504.

Please visit our website, www.enslowpublishing.com. For a free color catalog of all our high-quality books,
call toll free 1-800-398-2504 or fax 1-877-980-4454.

Cataloging-in-Publication Data

Names: Lowe, Lindsey.
Title: The story of Jesse James / Lindsey Lowe.
Description: New York: Enslow Publishing, 2024. | Series: On the run: true stories of legendary outlaws |
Includes glossary and index.
Identifiers: ISBN 9781978536746 (pbk.) | ISBN 9781978536753 (library bound) | ISBN 9781978536760 (ebook)
Subjects: James, Jesse, 1847-1882—Juvenile literature. | Outlaws—West (U.S.)—Biography—Juvenile
literature.| Frontier and pioneer life—West (U.S.)—Juvenile literature. | West (U.S.)—History—1860-1890—
Juvenile literature.
Classification: LCC F594.J27C66 2024 | 364.1552092—dc23

Find us on

CONTENTS

INTRODUCTION

Jesse James is famous as a feared outlaw of the Wild West. He was a bank robber, train robber, and murderer. He liked publicity and enjoyed involving the newspapers in his crimes.

Jesse James even left press releases at the scenes of some of his robberies. They told journalists how to report the crimes. Jesse saw himself as a kind of hero. He wanted others to see him as a hero, too. Jesse believed that he was standing up for the right of the states to ignore the U.S. government in Washington, DC. Many people agreed with him.

Jesse James was born on September 5, 1847, in Clay County, Missouri. At the time, U.S settlement was spreading west

This photograph, showing five generations of a family of enslaved people, was taken in South Carolina.

Jesse James grew up in Missouri. He and his family believed people should be allowed to enslave other people.

across North America. In 1803, the United States bought a huge region west of the Mississippi from France. The deal was called the Louisiana Purchase. It included the area that later became Missouri.

Political change

White settlers from the East Coast soon began to move into the new territory. They were looking for land to farm or the chance to set up a business, such as a store. In 1819, Missouri asked the U.S. government if it could become a state.

The request caused a problem for the U.S. government. The people in Missouri supported slavery. Like landowners in other Southern states, they wanted to use enslaved people to work on farms or plantations. However, people in northern and eastern states were against slavery.

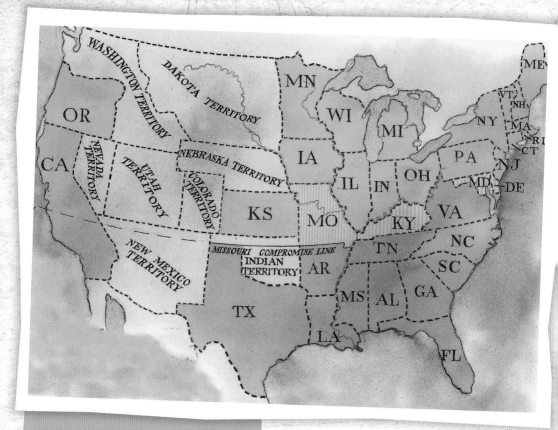

The country was divided into states that allowed slavery and free states. As territories became states, they chose whether to be free or to allow slavery.

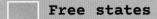
Free states

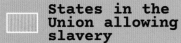
States in the Union allowing slavery

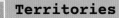
Territories

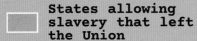
States allowing slavery that left the Union

If Missouri became a state, the states of the South allowing slavery would have more members in Congress than states that did not allow slavery. To keep the balance, Congress created the Missouri Compromise in 1820. This law separated Maine from Massachussetts to create a new "free" state. Missouri joined the Union as state allowing slavery in 1821. Congress also ruled that new states that joined the Union north of a certain line would ban slavery. It seemed the crisis had passed.

The Kansas-Nebraska Act

In 1854, the Kansas-Nebraska Act overturned the Missouri Compromise. The new law said that people living in the new states of Kansas and Nebraska could decide for themselves whether to be a state allowing slavery or a free state. In Kansas, many people opposed slavery, but many others supported it. The two sides clashed. There were violent fights.

Jesse James' family farm in Missouri lay close to the border with Kansas. The family followed stories about the growing violence in Kansas. They had a great effect on Jesse and his brother, Frank.

The James family farm where Jesse, his brother Frank, and their sister Susan Lavenia lived.

Frontier Upbringing

Jesse James grew up on the frontier. This was the very edge of the United States as white settlers moved westward across North America.

Life on the Frontier was often hard. There were few towns or stores, or services such as plumbing. Many people were poor farmers. They worked hard to make a living. Many people in Missouri used enslaved people to help them on their land.

Jesse's father, Robert James, was a farmer and a pastor at New Hope Baptist Church. He owned six enslaved people to help on his farm. In 1848, gold was discovered in California. Pastor James was one of the many people who rushed west to try to make his fortune.
He arrived in California

In 1842, Jesse's parents moved to this farm in Missouri from Kentucky. His father grew hemp, which was used to make rope.

early in 1850. By the summer he was dead from cholera.

Jesse's mother, Zerelda, remarried twice. Her second husband was a landowner, but he did not like Jesse or his brother, Frank. Zerelda's third husband was Dr. Reuben Samuel, whom she married in 1855. Later, he stopped practicing medicine to work on the family's hemp farm.

Supporting slavery

Like his father, Jesse believed people had the right to enslave people. His neighbors shared similar ideas. In 1854, men from Missouri crossed the border into Kansas. They voted illegally to allow slavery in the state. They did the same the next year. Opponents of slavery fought back.

ZERELDA JAMES

Zerelda (1825–1911) was a tough woman. She was known for having strong opinions. Zerelda supported the right to enslave people. She always believed Frank and Jesse were heroes and defended their reputations. After Jesse's death in 1882, she sold souvenirs of her son to people visiting his grave, but she tricked them by selling fake souvenirs.

Frank (left) and Jesse James photographed early in their career as outlaws.

FOCUS Bleeding Kansas

Kansas became a violent battleground between supporters and opponents of slavery. So much blood was spilled in the state that it became known as "Bleeding Kansas."

In the summer of 1855, about 1,200 people from New England moved to Kansas. They wanted to make sure that Kansas became a free state. Southerners also headed to Kansas to try to make sure it became a slave state. Many came from Missouri. They were described as "border ruffians." They crossed the border to vote illegally in Kansas elections. They also carried out raids to scare people in Kansas into voting to allow

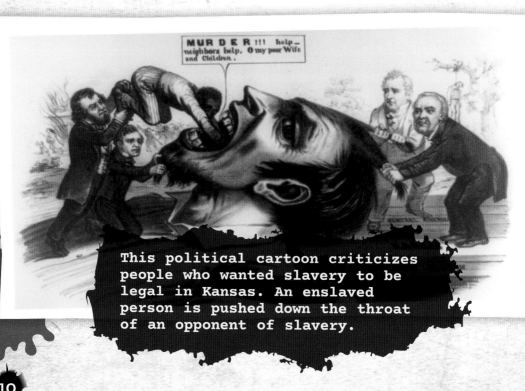

MURDER !!! help—neighbors help, O my poor Wife and Children.

This political cartoon criticizes people who wanted slavery to be legal in Kansas. An enslaved person is pushed down the throat of an opponent of slavery.

slavery. Things became so confused that Kansas had two governments for a time: one for slavery and one against slavery.

John Brown

The most famous person to arrive in Kansas to fight against slavery was an abolitionist named John Brown. He led a small band of raiders who attacked pro-slavery settlers in Kansas for months. At Pottawatomie, Brown's band killed five men.

Frank and Jesse James heard about these clashes. Jesse was too young to join in, but Frank was older. He may have joined the border ruffians. But Jesse James was old enough to know what was going on—and which side he was on.

JOHN BROWN

John Brown (1800–1859) believed slavery had to be stopped through violence. He fought against slavery in Kansas. In 1859, he led a raid on the federal armory at Harper's Ferry, Virginia, to get more weapons. He hoped to start a rebellion of enslaved people. Brown was captured, tried, and hanged. He became a hero to the whole abolitionist movement.

This drawing shows John Brown (center) meeting an enslaved woman and her baby on the way to his death.

11

FOCUS Bushwhackers

In 1861, the Civil War broke out. This set the Union, which vigorously opposed slavery, against the Confederate states, which equally vigorously supported it.

Alongside the regular armies, there were also groups of guerrillas on both sides. Both Frank and Jesse James joined bands of Confederate guerrillas known as "bushwhackers." Bushwhackers were groups of armed men. They mostly attacked families and farms in rural areas. They did not wear a uniform, but they saw themselves as a military force. Their opponents saw them as criminals who picked on those unable to defend themselves.

Quantrill's Raiders fight against U.S. Army soldiers they have trapped inside a house.

Bushwhackers led by William C. Quantrill attack Lawrence, Kansas, on August 21, 1863. They chose the town because most of its inhabitants opposed slavery.

Jesse joins in

Frank joined Quantrill's Raiders. The band was greatly feared. It attacked Union soldiers and opponents of slavery on the Kansas–Missouri border. On August 21, 1863, Frank James and 450 others raided Lawrence, Kansas. They murdered 183 men and boys. When Jesse James was sixteen, he joined the guerrilla leader "Bloody" Bill Anderson and his group of bushwhackers.

MASSACRE IN CENTRALIA

Jesse James was among the bushwhackers led by "Bloody" Bill Anderson who carried out one of the worst atrocities of the Civil War. On September 27, 1864, Anderson's men rode into the small Missouri town of Centralia. They executed 22 Union soldiers. Witnesses to this called the massacre a "carnival of blood."

Postwar Missouri

The Civil War ended in Union victory in 1865. However, Missouri's problems continued after the war.

In 1863 President Lincoln had freed all the enslaved people. The Republicans were in charge of Missouri. They began giving former enslaved people rights, such as the right to vote. This horrified former Confederates. The Republicans also punished those who had fought for the Southern states during the war. They took away their rights and brought in new laws. No one could vote unless they could prove they had not taken part in 86 different acts of rebellion during the Civil War.

The new laws left three-quarters of the white men in Jesse's home county unable to vote. Many people were unhappy. They resented the Union.

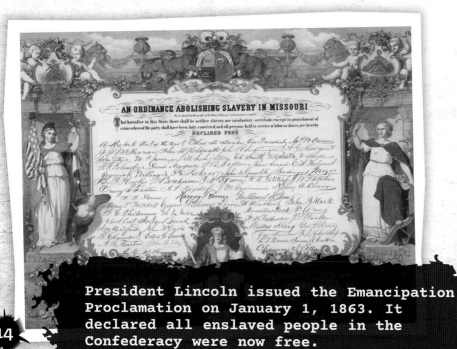

AN ORDINANCE ABOLISHING SLAVERY IN MISSOURI

President Lincoln issued the Emancipation Proclamation on January 1, 1863. It declared all enslaved people in the Confederacy were now free.

Fighting continues

Although the Civil War had ended, the fighting continued. Arguments about slavery did not go away. The bushwhackers continued to raid their enemies. An election was due to be held in Missouri in 1866. To impose order during the election, Governor Thomas Fletcher sent state militia to fight the bushwhackers.

Meanwhile, Jesse James was starting to make himself known. He wrote a letter to a newspaper.

VIOLENT TIMES

The fighting in Missouri was brutal. In some ways, it was like the fighting that had occurred between Native Americans and settlers a century before. Men fought each other hand to hand. Scalpings and stabbings were common, as were shootings. Missouri could be a very dangerous place.

St. Louis, the Missouri state capital, grew quickly after the end of the Civil War.

JESSE'S LETTER

In 1872, the *Kansas City Times* newspaper printed a letter from an anonymous outlaw. Most historians believe that the letter was written by Jesse James. It said: "Just let a party of men commit a bold robbery, and the cry is hang them, but Grant and his party can steal millions, and it is all right."

He pointed out that if one person robbed another, he would be punished with death. But, Jesse wrote, President Ulysses S. Grant and the Republicans were stealing millions of dollars from the South. They were not being punished at all.

A noble cause

In 1873 the Democrats took charge of Missouri from the Republicans. They set about reversing the laws that the Republicans had introduced. The Democrats believed that the Confederate cause during the Civil War had been a noble one. They argued that

This poster supports the former Union general Ulysses S. Grant for president. He was elected in 1868.

the South had been defeated in the war because the Union was powerful and wealthy. The cause itself was still worth fighting for. The Democrats opposed attempts at Reconstruction. They believed the North wanted to destroy the Southern way of life.

A moral right

Against this background, Jesse James decided that he did not have to obey the laws imposed by the government in Washington, D.C. In fact, he believed that he had a moral right to attack any enemies of the Confederacy. They included businesses based in the North. He saw this not as becoming a criminal but becoming a hero. Jesse decided to turn to a life of crime. His brother Frank joined him. It was not long before they committed their first robbery.

Volunteers run a sewing class for once-enslaved people at the end of the Civil War. Democrats did not want to give the former enslaved people any rights.

First Crime?

Jesse James was likely involved in his first robbery in 1866, when he was with Archie Clement's bushwacker gang.

On February 13, 1866, Archie Clement and his gang carried out a raid. They robbed the Clay County Savings Bank in Liberty, Missouri. It was the first ever daytime bank robbery in America.

Daring raid

The Clay County Savings Bank was owned and run by Republicans, so it was a target for the bushwhackers. The raiders pistol-whipped the cashier. They stole as much as $58,000 in bonds, paper money, gold, and silver coins. As they escaped, a passerby was shot dead.

Frank (left) and Jesse James with Zerelda.

The raid seemed to have been carried out by bushwhackers, but the precise identity of the robbers has never been confirmed. However, historians believe Jesse James was one of them. Eyewitnesses in Liberty later came forward. They identified both Frank and Jesse James as being among the members of the gang.

The authorities believed that Archie Clement was responsible. They hunted him down. Clement was finally shot dead by state militia in Lexington, Kentucky, on December 13, 1866.

LONG CAREER

Based on the length of his career, Jesse James was one of the most successful bank robbers in American history. It took 15 years before he was captured. In that time, he put together a number of different gangs. But his robberies rarely went as planned. In many ways, he was lucky to get away with it for as long as he did.

The Clay County Savings Bank still stands in Liberty, Missouri.

Fame for Jesse and Frank

Jesse finally received the publicity he wanted. During a raid in Gallatin, Missouri, he shot and killed a bank teller.

On December 7, 1869, Frank and Jesse robbed the Daviess County Savings Bank in Gallatin, Missouri. It is the first robbery where it is known for certain Frank and Jesse were involved. The cashier, John W. Sheets, was writing out a receipt for changing a $100 bill when Jesse shot him dead. Jesse grabbed some money as the brothers escaped. They left town chased by a posse. The money Jesse had taken was worth less than $1,000.

The James Gang robbed their first bank in the small town of Gallatin, Missouri.

THE WRONG MAN

At Gallatin, Jesse thought he was shooting Samuel P. Cox. Cox was a member of the militia who had killed "Bloody" Bill Anderson. Anderson had been a member of Quantrill's Raiders. He also led his own gang. He killed many Union men in Kansas and Missouri during the Civil War. Anderson died when Cox shot him in a gunfight.

PROCLAMATION

OF THE

GOVERNOR OF MISSOURI!

REWARDS

FOR THE ARREST OF

Express and Train Robbers.

STATE OF MISSOURI,
EXECUTIVE DEPARTMENT.

WHEREAS, It has been made known to me, as the Governor of the State of Missouri, that certain parties, whose names are to me unknown, have confederated and banded themselves together for the purpose of committing robberies and other depredations within this State; and

WHEREAS, Said parties did, on or about the Eighth day of October, 1879, stop a train near Glendale, in the county of Jackson, in said State, and, with force and violence, take, steal and carry away the money and other express matter being carried thereon; and

WHEREAS, On the fifteenth day of July 1881, said parties and their confederates did stop a train upon the lines of the Chicago, Rock Island and Pacific Railroad, near Winston, in the County of Daviess, in said State, and, with force and violence, take, steal, and carry away the money and other express matter being carried thereon; and, in perpetration of the robbery last aforesaid, the parties engaged therein did kill and murder one WILLIAM WESTFALL, the conductor of the train, together with one JOHN MCCULLOCH, who was at the time in the employ of said company, then on said train; and

WHEREAS, FRANK JAMES and JESSE W. JAMES stand indicted in the Circuit Court of said Daviess County, for the murder of JOHN W. SHEETS, and

NOW, THEREFORE, in consideration of the premises, and in lieu of all other rewards heretofore offered for the arrest or conviction of the parties aforesaid, or either of them, by any person or corporation, I, THOMAS T. CRITTENDEN, Governor of the State of Missouri, do hereby offer a reward of five thousand dollars ($5,000.00) for the arrest and conviction of each person participating in either of the robberies or murders aforesaid, excepting the said FRANK JAMES and JESSE W. JAMES; and for the arrest and delivery of said

FRANK JAMES and JESSE W. JAMES,

and each or either of them, to the sheriff of said Daviess County, I hereby offer a reward of five thousand dollars, ($5,000.00,) and for the conviction of either party last aforesaid of participation in either of the murders or robberies above mentioned, I hereby offer a further reward of five thousand dollars, ($5,000.00,)

IN TESTIMONY WHEREOF, I have hereunto set my hand and caused to be affixed the Great Seal of the State of Missouri. Done at the City of Jefferson on this 28th day of July, A. D. 1881.

[SEAL.]

THOS. T. CRITTENDEN.

By the Governor:
MICHL. K. McGRATH, Sec'y of State.

As Frank and Jesse robbed more banks and trains, the rewards offered for their arrest increased.

Notoriety

It turned out that Jesse had killed John W. Sheets because he thought Sheets was a man named Samuel P. Cox. He had killed Jesse's old bushwhacker commander, "Bloody" Bill Anderson. Like many of Jesse's robberies, things had not gone according to plan.

The Gallatin robbery was the first time Jesse's name had been definitely linked with a crime. The governor of Missouri offered a cash reward for the capture of Jesse and Frank. They were now officially outlaws.

Household Name

Jesse loved seeing his name in print. He rapidly became a celebrity thanks to a journalist for the *Kansas City Times*.

John Newman Edwards was editor of the *Kansas City Times*. He was a former officer in the Confederate Army. He wanted to get supporters of the Southern cause back into power. He thought Jesse James could help.

Robin Hood?

Six months after the Gallatin raid, Edwards published a letter from Jesse. Jesse argued that Union men were the real criminals, not the James brothers. In 1873, Edwards used 20 pages of the *St. Louis Dispatch* to praise Jesse's exploits. He made Jesse seem like a modern-day Robin Hood, the English outlaw who was said to have stood up for ordinary people against authority.

This photograph of Jesse with his gun helped to promote his outlaw image.

This newspaper report prints a letter from Jesse protesting that he is innocent of a recent robbery.

Jesse was pleased with the image Edwards created for him. Later he even named his own son after Edwards.

Jesse started to leave press releases at his crime scenes to ensure he received good publicity. He carried a copy of the Bible on his raids. That reinforced the idea that even though he was an outlaw he had right on his side.

ROBIN HOOD

Robin Hood was a legendary English outlaw in the Middle Ages. He led a band of outlaws who lived in Sherwood Forest in central England. Robin Hood claimed that he only robbed the rich to help the poor. No one is certain that Robin Hood was a real person.

Outlaw Brothers in Arms

In 1868, Frank and Jesse James joined forces with another group of outlaws to form the notorious James-Younger gang.

The four Younger brothers were Cole, John, Jim, and Bob. They formed the core of the gang, with Frank and Jesse James. Other members joined at times. They included Clell Miller and other former Confederate bushwhackers. Jesse was the best known of the gang. Everyone thought he was the leader. In fact, the six main members shared power and made important decisions together.

Public support

The newspaperman John Newman Edwards continued to report news about the gang, portraying them as Confederate heroes. The gang still received support from the public.

This photograph shows Bob (left), Cole (front, center), and Jim Younger, with their sister.

The two sets of brothers moved freely around their homes in Missouri. No one turned the gang in to the authorities. In fact, the public even helped to hide them from the law. This made it very difficult to catch them.

In the early 1870s, the gang became more active. They robbed stagecoaches, banks, and even a fair in Kansas City. They also began robbing trains in the states of Missouri, Iowa, Louisiana, and Arkansas.

OFF THE RAILS

The James-Younger gang robbed their first train on July 21, 1873. They derailed the Rock Island train in Adair, Iowa, and made off with $3,000. They often only robbed the guard's wagon, where valuables were kept. They usually left the passengers alone.

There were growing numbers of trains in the West. They became targets for gangs of robbers.

Growing Reputation

The James and Younger brothers became increasingly confident. They raided over larger areas and Jesse's fame spread.

The outlaws became more daring in their robberies. In June 1871 the James-Younger gang arrived in Corydon, Iowa. Most of the town was at the local Methodist church. They were listening to a popular speaker named Henry Clay Dean. He was an outspoken critic of the Civil War and the late President Abraham Lincoln. While everyone was inside the church, the gang raided the Corydon State Bank, robbing it of a sum in the region of $6,000.

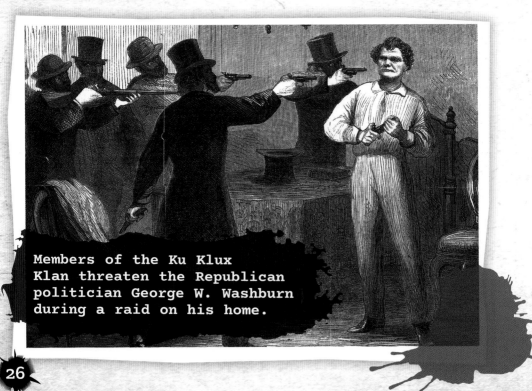

Members of the Ku Klux Klan threaten the Republican politician George W. Washburn during a raid on his home.

Instead of running away, the James-Younger gang went to the church. They shouted out that they had robbed the bank. They also shouted "Catch us if you can." Then they left town.

The gang began to carry out raids as far south as Texas and as far east as West Virginia. In April 1872, they raided another bank in Columbia, Kentucky, and killed an unarmed cashier.

KU KLUX KLAN

The Ku Klux Klan was formed in the 1860s. Its members wore hoods to keep their identity secret. They harassed former enslaved people to stop them from voting for the Republicans. Members of the Klan beat or even killed African Americans.

Bank robberies

The gang was growing more ambitious. They were not frightened of being arrested because there was little law and order in the West. It was a violent place. An organization called the Ku Klux Klan had emerged to resist the federal government. Many former Confederate soldiers were members. They set about attacking former enslaved people.

The Confederate general Nathan Bedford Forrest was a founder of the Ku Klux Klan.

FOCUS The Railroads

In 1865, the Civil War ended and more people headed west to settle. Private companies built railroads to make travel safer and more comfortable.

People in the South feared that the railroads would bring Northern laws and Northern settlers to their land. They saw the railroads as proof that the North was trying to control the whole country. Railroad building had started in 1828 with the construction of the Baltimore and Ohio Railroad. By 1860, every city in the North and Midwest was on a railroad. After the Civil War ended in 1865, the railroads headed west.

In the years leading up to the Civil War and after it ended, railroads were built across the country.

This picture of a train yard shows passenger cars and boxcars used for carrying other cargo.

Booming railroads

For ordinary people, the railroads were a huge advance. Previously, long journeys had to be made by horse or stagecoach. Both were a dangerous and uncomfortable way to travel. The new trains were luxurious in comparison. Trains also carried goods such as grain, hogs, cattle, and money. It was the money that interested the James-Younger gang. They usually left any passengers alone.

Catch Jesse!

With attacks on their trains increasing, the railroad companies took action. They hired the Pinkerton detective agency to catch the outlaws.

On the afternoon of January 31, 1874, the Little Rock Express train approached Gads Hill. The town was 100 miles (160 km) south of St. Louis. It had a population of just 15. The James-Younger Gang was waiting there. They were all wearing Ku Klux Klan hoods. They had rounded up and robbed the town's residents, and they stopped and robbed the train, getting away with over $6,000. The Adams Express Company owned the train. It wanted the outlaws caught.

The Pinkerton National Detective Agency became the largest private security firm in the world.

The Pinkertons

Allan Pinkerton had founded a detective agency in 1850. The railroad hired it to catch the gang. The agency sent John W. Whicher to track Jesse down in March 1874. Whicher arrived in Clay County as an under cover agent. He asked about

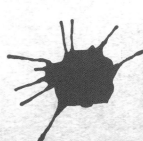

Allan Pinkerton (seated, right) and some of his agents photographed during the Civil War.

Jesse. The next day, Whicher was found shot dead. There was a note with the body. It threatened anyone asking about Jesse and Frank with the same fate.

Allan Pinkerton now took charge of catching the gang. His agents fought a gun battle with the Younger brothers. John Younger was fatally shot, as was an agent. Allan Pinkerton swore he would get even.

PRESS RELEASE

The gang handed printed notes to passengers at Gads Hill. It read: "The robbers were all large men, none of them under six feet tall. They were all masked. They were all mounted on fine blooded horses. There's ... excitement in this part of the country."

Raid on the Family Home

Worse was to follow for Pinkerton. A raid by his agents on the James family farm did not go to plan.

Allan Pinkerton was outraged by the deaths of two of his agents. He decided to catch the James brothers by surprise at their home. He led a raid on the family farm on January 25, 1875.

Disaster strikes!

Pinkerton agents and a posse from Clay County surrounded the farm. They threw a bomb made from a hollow iron ball filled with flammable jelly through a window. The bomb exploded in the fireplace. Shrapnel from the bomb killed Jesse's half-brother, Archie, and injured his mother, Zerelda. She lost part

Today, the James family farm is a historic site. Jesse is buried in the front yard.

This illustration shows Jesse fighting off the attackers. In reality, he was not even home.

of her right arm. But neither Frank nor Jesse was home. Pinkerton had once again failed to catch them.

The bombing of the family farm resulted in renewed support for the gang. Missouri politicians tried to pass a bill offering the brothers an amnesty, but the bill was narrowly defeated. Meanwhile, the James brothers began to hunt down and kill any people who helped the Pinkerton agency.

GIVING UP

The raid on the farm was the end of Allan Pinkerton's pursuit of Jesse James. He did not try to catch him again. Instead, the Pinkerton agency began working for coal and steel companies. The agents helped discover plans for strikes. They also used violence against striking workers.

The Final Target

When John Younger was killed, Frank was keen to retire but Jesse had other ideas. He wanted to carry on robbing banks.

In the summer of 1876, the James-Younger gang decided to rob a bank in Minnesota. On September 7, 1876, the gang arrived in the town of Northfield, Minnesota. Their target was the First National Bank.

Poor planning

The gang split into three. Jesse, Frank, and Bob Younger were to rob the bank. Another group would act as lookout. The third group was to cover a getaway. The gang agreed that no civilians were to be hurt. The raid went wrong from the start. No one inside the bank would open the safe. Outside, Northfield's storekeepers grew suspicious of the lookout team. Soon, some of the residents became involved in a deadly shootout with the gang.

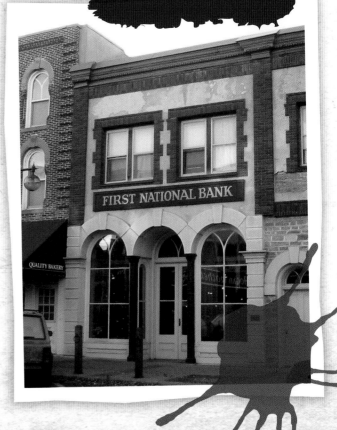

The First National Bank in Northfield was the target for the James-Younger gang's last raid.

These guns were used by Jesse and his gang. They were displayed in a museum in the 1920s.

HANDS OFF, PLEASE

Escape!

All the gang members except Jesse were either wounded or killed. Jesse and the wounded men fled, chased by the citizens of Northfield. For the next two weeks, the gang tried to get away to safety. Eventually, the James brothers split up from the others. They headed to Tennessee, where Jesse was living. That event was to mark the end of the James-Younger gang.

CITIZEN LAW

The people of Northfield had succeeded where law agencies had failed. They ended the 15-year reign of Jesse and his gang. Many of the citizens were Civil War veterans. Some had fought the Sioux during clashes with the Native Americans in 1862. Many of them were also deer hunters. They all knew how to handle a gun.

Jesse's New Gang

After Northfield, the brothers kept their heads down. It had been the last straw for Frank, who retired. But Jesse was restless.

Both James brothers moved to Tennessee. They lived under false names. Frank called himself B. J. Woods and Jesse used the name J. D. Howard. Jesse tried to make a living by racing horses and playing cards but he was a poor gambler. Soon he was running out of money.

Another gang

Jesse also missed being in the public eye. In the summer of 1879, he returned to Missouri to form a new gang. The gang carried out violent robberies in Missouri and the South. But Jesse no longer had public support.

Jesse and Frank James settled in small Western towns where they could remain anonymous.

In this drawing from the time, the James-Younger gang rob people on a train.

Jesse's long-time champion, the newspaper editor John Newman Edwards, had also turned against him. He ignored Jesse's crimes, giving them no publicity.

By early 1882, Jesse was living in Missouri with his wife, Zee, and their two young children. He was putting together yet another gang. But he no longer trusted its members. He even murdered one of them, Ed Miller. The only people Jesse now trusted were the brothers Robert and Charley Ford.

NEW RECRUITS

Jesse's new gang members lacked the experience of the original gang. They were not as loyal to Jesse, either. Without his brother, Frank, and without public support, Jesse did not seem like a Robin Hood figure anymore. He was not fighting for a noble cause. He was like any other violent criminal.

Trusted Traitor

Jesse James had no idea the man he most trusted would be his killer. Robert Ford saw Jesse as a hero, but money changed his mind.

Robert, or Bob, Ford was the youngest of seven children. His older brother, Charley, joined Jesse James's new gang. He may have taken part in the Blue Cut train robbery of September 7, 1881. Growing up, Bob had admired what he heard about Jesse. He was eager to meet his hero.

Bob joins the gang

Bob Ford met Jesse for the first time in 1880. At the time, Bob was nineteen. By 1881, the Ford brothers were living close to Jesse and his family in Missouri. Jesse soon came to feel that he could trust the Fords. When Jesse wanted to commit a new crime, he asked the Ford brothers to take part in a robbery in Platte City. The brothers turned down the offer. They had other plans.

Bob Ford betrayed the man who trusted him in return for money and a pardon for his crimes.

A new governor

Thomas T. Crittenden had just been elected governor of Missouri. During the election campaign, he promised to bring the James brothers to justice. Bob Ford met with the governor on January 13, 1882. He got Crittenden to promise the Ford brothers a full pardon and a reward if they killed Jesse.

Crittenden had persuaded the railroad companies to offer a reward of $10,000 for each James brother, dead or alive. Frank had retired to West Virginia. Bob convinced Charley Ford that they had to kill Jesse. It was just a question of when.

By 1882, Jesse's latest gang had fallen apart. Dick Liddil, helped by Bob Ford, had shot Jesse's cousin. Jesse had killed Ed Miller for talking too much about their crimes. However, he was still convinced that he could trust the Ford brothers. He even invited them to live with his family.

CRIME FIGHTER

When Thomas T. Crittenden became governor, Missouri had a reputation in the rest of the country for lawlessness. He explained his intention to fight crime in his first speech. He said, "Missouri cannot be the home and abiding place of lawlessness of any character."

Governor Crittenden was determined to bring law and order to Missouri.

Shot in the Head

Bob and Charley Ford soon made history. They grabbed their chance for fame and fortune and killed the famous outlaw.

Jesse James was always armed. He almost never took off his pistol. The Ford brothers knew they would lose any gunfight against him. They waited for a chance to catch him off guard.

On the morning of April 3, 1882, Jesse's wife, Zee, was cooking breakfast. Jesse was getting ready for a robbery. The Ford brothers were also in the house.

Fatal shot

As Jesse went in and out of the house, he got warm and took off his coat. In order not to draw attention to himself while he was outside, Jesse also took off his pistols. Returning inside, he then climbed onto a chair to clean a picture.

Bob Ford shoots Jesse. Shooting a man from behind was seen as the act of a coward.

THE HOUSE IN WHICH JESSE JAMES → WAS KILLED.

THE HOME OF FRANK & JESSE JAMES

THE BAPTIST CHURCH KEARNEY MO. IN WHICH THE FUNERAL SERVICES WERE HELD.

The Ford brothers drew their guns. Bob shot Jesse at point blank range in the back of the head. Jesse James was dead!

This postcard appeared after Jesse's death. It shows key places in his life.

Pardon and Reward

The Ford brothers gave themselves up at once. They were charged with murder but Governor Crittenden kept his word. He pardoned them. The brothers also received some of the reward money they had been promised, but not all of it.

PUBLIC OUTCRY

After the murder, Bob Ford tried to make a career out of his new fame. He re-enacted the shooting and posed for photographs. But the public was outraged at the cowardly nature of Jesse's killing. Bob Ford had to flee Missouri for his own safety. He was shot dead in 1892 by Edward O'Kelley. Charley Ford took his own life.

FOCUS Legacy

Jesse had always craved publicity. Even after his death, his fame lived on. He was celebrated as a romantic outlaw, not as a cold-blooded killer.

In the movie *The Assassination of Jesse James by the Coward Robert Ford* (2007), Jesse was played by Brad Pitt (front, left).

Jesse James lived at a time when the West was opening up. People on the East Coast read cheap paperback books known as "dime novels." They loved reading about the daring things that happened in the West. Authors were quick to write exaggerated accounts of Jesse's exploits. Jesse became famous everywhere.

Jesse lives on

Jesse's family also cashed in on his fame. His mother had him buried in her front yard. She sold pebbles from his grave to people who came to see the famous outlaw's final resting place. When they ran out, she sold pebbles from her backyard.

Frank James gave himself up to Governor Crittenden five months after Jesse died. He briefly tried to cash in on his fame. He joined a touring show called the Buckskin Bill Wild West Show, but soon quit.

Jesse's son, Jesse Jr., wrote a book entitled *Jesse James, My Father*. The only family member who did not cash in on Jesse's name was his wife, Zee. She refused an offer to write a book.

The first movie about Jesse was made in 1908. Since then, Hollywood has been fascinated by the outlaw. Jesse has featured in countless films and stories as an example of a "noble bandit."

HERO OR THUG?

Some people saw Jesse as a hero of the Southern cause. He saw himself in this way, as a romantic bandit. Other people saw him as an ordinary criminal and murderer. Jesse was certainly a pioneer: he was the first true bank robber. No one had robbed a bank before the James gang raids.

W.I. SWAIN'S WESTERN SPECTACULAR PRODUCTION
JESSE JAMES.

This is a poster for a show based on Jesse's life that was popular during the 1880s.

Rogues' Gallery

Jesse was the most famous outlaw of his time, but he was not the only one. There were other outlaws operating in the "Wild West." Some rode with Jesse.

Archie Clement (1846–1866)

"Little Arch" was a pro-Confederate guerrilla leader and bushwhacker. He was known for his violent attacks on Union soldiers. He and the James brothers carried out the 1866 bank raid in Liberty, Missouri. Clement died in a gun battle with state militia soon afterward.

Belle Starr (1848–1889)

Belle grew up with the James brothers in Missouri. She was known for her skill at shooting and horse riding. Belle helped rustlers, bootleggers, and anyone outside of the law. She married a Cherokee, Sam Starr (left). They settled down in Indian territory.

Cole Younger
(1844–1916)

Thomas Coleman "Cole" Younger fought with Quantrill's Raiders during the Civil War. When peace returned, Cole and some of his brothers may have joined Archie Clement's gang. The first robbery in which Cole definitely took part was in 1868, when the Younger brothers—Cole, John, Jim, and Bob—first teamed up with the James brothers. In September 1876, Cole, Bob, and Jim Younger were captured after robbing a bank in Northfield, Missouri, and sentenced to prison for life. Cole was released in 1901, after serving nearly 25 years in prison.

"Bloody" Bill Anderson
(1840–1864)

William T. Anderson was a pro-Confederate guerrilla who rode with Quantrill's Raiders. After he fell out with Quantrill, Anderson formed his own gang, which Jesse James joined. In September 1864 Anderson's men captured a train in Centralia, Missouri. They killed 24 Union soldiers on board; later that day they ambushed and killed 100 more Union soldiers. A month later, a Union soldier named Samuel P. Cox shot Anderson dead in a gunfight.

Glossary

Abolitionist Someone who tried to make slavery against the law.

Amnesty A pardon for a crime.

Cholera A fatal disease that is usually caught by drinking infected water.

Compromise A solution to a dispute in which each side makes concessions to the other.

Federal Relating to the central government rather than to state or local government.

Guerillas People who fight an enemy by using tactics such as ambushes or assassination.

Justice A word for having to face the law and the consequences of breaking it.

Militia Citizen soldiers who are called on to fight in times of emergency or danger.

Pistol-whipped Hit someone with a gun as if it were a club.

Point Blank When a bullet is fired very close to its target.

Posse A group of citizens organized by a sheriff in order to enforce the law.

Reconstruction The period from 1865 to 1877 when the government imposed conditions on the losing Southern states at the end of the Civil War.

Safe A strong fireproof box or room with a complex lock for storing valuables.

Shrapnel Fragments of a bomb sprayed out by an explosion.

Undercover Taking on a different identity to gather information in a community.

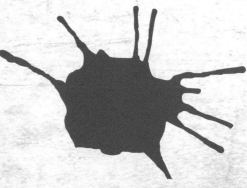

Further Resources

Books

Captivating History. *Jesse James: A Captivating Guide to a Wild West Outlaw Who Robbed Trains, Banks, and Stagecoaches across the Midwestern United States.* Captivating History, 2020.

Captivating History. *The Wild West: A Captivating uide to the American Old West, Including Stories of Famous Outlaws and Lawmen Such as Billy the Kid, Pat Garret, Wyatt Earp, Wild Bill Hickok, and More.* Captivating History, 2021.

London, Martha. *Fact and Fiction of the Wild West.* Core Library, an imprint of Abdo Publishing, 2021.

Walton, Kathryn. *The Emancipation Proclamation.* Enslow Publishing, 2024.

Websites

www.historicmissourians.shsmo. org/jesse-james
Pages from the Historic Missourians site, with photographs, and links to pages for futher research.

www.history.com/news/history-lists/7-things-you-might-not-know-about-jesse-james
A list of surprising facts about Jesse James from History.com.

www.legendsofamerica.com/we-jessejames.html
Page from Old West Legends that asks, "Jesse James – folklore hero or cold-blooded killer?"

www.biography.com/crime-figure/jesse-james
Pages about Jesse James from biography.com.

Publisher's note to educators and parents: Our editors have carefully reviewed these websites to ensure that they are suitable for students. Many websites change frequently, however, and we cannot guarantee that a site's future contents will continue to meet our high standards of quality and educational value. Be advised that students should be closely supervised whenever they access the Internet.

INDEX

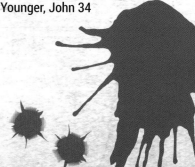